The Ideal Classroom Setting for the Selectively Mute Child

Written and designed by:

Dr. Elisa Shipon-Blum
President & Director: Selective Mutism Anxiety Research & Treatment Center
(SMART-Center) Philadelphia, Pennsylvania
Founder & Director Emeritus Selective Mutism Group Childhood Anxiety Network
Clinical Asst Professor Psychology & Family Medicine
Philadelphia College Osteopathic Medicine

Edited by:
Adrienne Wallage (First Edition)
Dr. Christine Stanley (Second Edition)
Sharon Longo (Second Edition)

Selective Mutism Anxiety Research & Treatment Center Publishing
(SMART-Center) Philadelphia, Pennsylvania

First published 2001, Revised edition 2003, Reprinted and revised July 2007

Copyright Rev. 2007 by Dr. Elisa Shipon-Blum

ISBN 0-9714800-0-1

INDEX

"I dedicate this book to all the teachers, treating professionals and parents who need guidance in setting up the 'Ideal classroom' setting for the Selectively Mute child" Elisa Shipon-Blum DO

INTRODUCTION
A note from the author

Selective Mutism (SM) is a childhood anxiety disorder where a child cannot speak in select settings, such as in school, despite his/her ability to speak in situations where the child is comfortable, such as at home. School is often the most difficult place for the child with Selective Mutism. Since over 95% of SM children have social anxiety, the school setting can be extremely anxiety provoking. In addition, what other location places a greater expectation on a child then the school setting? From the minute the child enters the school building there is an expectation for certain behaviors and performance.

Being unable to communicate verbally can be quite debilitating and painful for the child and family affected. These children often stand motionless with fear as they are confronted with specific social settings. This can be quite heart wrenching to watch. These children are so anxious they appear to freeze; they may be expressionless, seem unemotional and literally suffer in silence as the world goes on around them. As children with SM get older, the 'frozen, stone-faced look' may start to dissipate, but unlike in preschool and early elementary years where peers are often accepting of their silence, older elementary children and teens may become socially isolated and withdrawn from most classmates and peers.

It is important to understand that although environmental stressors play an important role in anxiety and other mood disorders, most children with SM have a hereditary predisposition to anxiety disorders, and as mentioned, the majority of children also have social phobia. What needs to be clear is that the Selectively Mute child's inability to communicate effectively is a DIRECT RESULT of inner anxiety and the subconscious defense of avoiding anxious feelings brought on by an expectation for speech and communication. Children suffering from Selective Mutism are not choosing to be silent nor refusing to speak, nor are they being oppositional in a purposeful manner. They have developed dysfunctional coping skills to combat anxiety.

Without a doubt, Selective Mutism (SM) is THE MOST misdiagnosed, mismanaged and mistreated anxiety disorder of childhood. Children with Selective Mutism truly suffer in silence, and yet most people completely misunderstand the child's silence. Reasons for this vary from lack of awareness to inaccurate and misleading information in the medical and educational literature. Because of this, mutism and anxiety often persist and intensify until the child is either seen correctly and receives proper treatment, or anxiety persists and ramifications of untreated anxiety prevail; these include social isolation, poor school performance or drop out, self-medication with drugs and alcohol, inability to seek employment as an adult, and in extreme cases even suicide.

What is crucial to understand is that NO child truly wants to be MUTE, yet so many others see SM children as controlling and manipulative in their silence. To date, I have rarely met a truly oppositional SM child. I have seen children develop oppositional qualities, but in my professional opinion, these tendencies develop as a result of defense and insecurity over their inability to 'get the words out.' Something as easy as speaking is virtually impossible for the anxious SM child. How degrading, frustrating, and embarrassing, not to mention contributing to the development of low self esteem.

A teacher recently commented that she can SEE and HEAR the SM child speaking quite normally directly outside the room or immediately as the child gets into his parents' car. Defiance, control and oppositional behavior are the first things that came to this teacher's mind. However, I believe her assumption is markedly incorrect. This teacher should consider that the anxiety level for the child drastically changed from one setting to another. Just moving from one location to another or being in the presence of a specific person is enough to make a huge difference to this child

As children get older, defense mechanisms become blatant. Children may state that they 'do not want to speak,' "do not have anything to say', can't speak' but 'will speak in the future.' These statements are a direct reflection of the child's inability to speak in various settings and their 'subconscious' attempt to rationalize their disability. How frustrating and incapacitating to be able to speak and communicate with ease in one situation, yet become paralyzed and perhaps non-communicative in another setting. To make matters worse, SM children may be able to chatter nonstop to one person in one setting, yet become communicatively inept in another! Therefore, seeing the SM child as anxious and stifled, rather than difficult, controlling and oppositional will enable our children to be diagnosed early and treated effectively to overcome their disability and flourish academically, socially and emotionally.

Before discussing the truths about SM and how to create the Ideal Classroom Setting for the SM child, it is of utmost importance to explain the biggest misconceptions that others have about the SM child's mutism and inability to communicate properly. This is crucial, since many school personnel, treating professionals and parents who are reading this book may indeed realize that their student/patient/child is being misunderstood.

Children with Selective Mutism are often viewed as:

(1) '<u>**Just shy**</u>' – This is the typical SM child who enters school mute or 'near mute' and has a difficult time making eye contact and interacting with other children/ adults. This child withdraws from interaction initially, but may warm up and participate after an indeterminate amount of time. This child has been labeled as shy by their parents, teachers and friends. In many cases, mutism persists from year to year. Parents are told by their doctors, teachers, therapists, school administrators, psychologists and counselors that the child will 'outgrow their quietness' and to hold tight! Unfortunately, for the child who truly has SM, this advice could not be more inappropriate. Years often go by, and although some of these children may begin to 'squeak out' a word or two, their SM begins to manifest more as social anxiety.

(2) **Autistic** - This is the SEVERE SM child who is so anxious that he/she stands motionless and expressionless with a blank look on his/her face. This child is unable to respond or initiate nonverbally as well as verbally. Standardized testing is inaccurate since the child is unable to point or nod, and is unable to initiate due to heightened anxiety. However, if the parents are questioned about the child's behavior at home, or if videotapes of the child at home could be viewed, it would become clear that this 'autistic-acting' child in school is anything but withdrawn and noncommunicative at home. On the contrary, like most SM children, this child is verbal, interactive, engaging and sensitive. In fact, he/she is often boisterous and assertive! Unfortunately though, many of these children are never seen correctly and are placed in special classes designed for children with Pervasive Developmental Delays. Their educational plan is directed toward the treatment of autism. Many of these children go through their entire school career completely mismanaged.

(3) **Oppositional and Defiant** - This may be the child who will say, 'I don't talk,' 'I don't want to talk' or 'I can't talk at school.' These children often have negative behaviors at home and at school. WHY? Because this child has a wall of defense that is preventing him/her from acknowledging and accepting his/her anxiety. This child is frustrated and, because so few truly understand, the wall of defense becomes thicker and thicker and, unless addressed, the child may become increasingly more isolated and more 'difficult.'

(4) **Selectively Mute** - Fortunately, this child has the correct diagnosis! However, many diagnosed SM children are still not approached correctly. This child is being bribed, begged and pleaded with to speak. Parents and teachers may be incorrectly advised to have a firm expectation for the child to speak in all situations. This child may have privileges taken away or withheld because he/she is not speaking. This child's mutism is becoming ingrained and self esteem is being damaged. Mutism and anxiety will persist and most likely intensify until the correct approach (hopefully!) is taken by the parents, school and treating professional.

Obviously, the attitude towards SM, by the individuals involved with the child, will dictate the manner in which the SM child's silence is understood. For example, parents are told
That their child is not talking and school administrators, psychologists, doctors or therapists state to the parents and teachers that mutism is a form of:
- autism
- oppositional behavior
- or a manifestation of shyness

Others will then continue to see the child in this light. As a result, the seemingly endless journey continues and the child's anxiety only persists. It should not be surprising that for the 'typical SM' child, mutism becomes learned and ingrained, and the longer mutism persists, the more difficult it is to overcome. Therefore, the younger the anxious and mute child is when diagnosis and appropriate treatment is begun, the easier it will be to overcome Selective Mutism.

To truly understand the child who suffers in silence and to be able to help this child, teachers, treating professionals and parents need to see SM in the correct light. From working with hundreds of SM children I am confident to state that SM is, without a doubt, a form of **social communication anxiety.**

Bearing this in mind, it must be understood that the typical SM child cannot go from mutism (severe social communication anxiety) to speaking (greatly reduced social communication anxiety) easily. There are various stages of communication that the SM child will go through in order to progress and become a confident and social verbally communicative child.

The degree of social communication anxiety needs to be determined in various settings (can the child communicate nonverbally, verbally or does the child stand motionless when approached?) as well as the depth of anxiety that exists from one setting to another (In how many settings is the child mute and in what settings can the child verbally communicate with other children/adults?)

I have developed the **SM-Stages of Social Communication Comfort Scale** (SM-SCCS) (see page 8) as a means of assessing the "Stage" of anxiety that the SM child is in from one setting to another. Suggestions would be for parent, teacher and treating professional to work together to determine which stages the child is in within various school settings in order to help him/her progress communicatively   Use of this scale will help with determining goals to enable for communication progression.

It should be noted that the SM child's anxiety will change from situation to situation and person to person. It should also be noted that initiating nonverbally is difficult for most SM children. For example, Child A can be talkative, chatty and assertive with her best friend at home and outside of school (Stage 3B) but is nonverbal and unable to communicate initiate (Stage 0) when in school. Or, Child B can hand money to a store clerk, but is unable to hand a note to her teacher.

In other words, classic SM behavior is anxiety that changes across settings. Perhaps this is one of the factors leading to misunderstanding, because of the belief that the child SHOULD be consistent from one setting to the next. This perpetual belief will only halt progress and cause greater anxiety in our SM children.

Selective mutism is an anxiety disorder and needs to be approached from an anxiety perspective. For the child to successfully overcome SM, certain characteristics must be present within the classroom to enable for the development of social comfort and progression of communication

There are various tactics that can be used to help a child progress through the stages of communication, once an accurate assessment is made of the child's status. One such tactic, a verbal intermediary (Transitional Stage- Stage 2), is someone or something that is used "as an agent" to transfer the child's spoken word into a new environment or towards a person with whom the child was previously mute. For some children, the use of the verbal intermediary is crucial, whereas other children (usually the younger preschool children) may spontaneously enter into Stage 3 with basic tactics and techniques.

Goals for parents, teachers and treating professionals are to work together in a purposeful manner to HELP the SM child overcome his/her difficulty with communication by providing the *ideal classroom setting* which promotes:

(1) Lowered Anxiety
(2) Building of self-esteem
(3) Increased social comfort
(4) Progression of Communication

This is accomplished with a <u>team approach;</u> the team consisting of the SM child, the parents, school personnel, and an experienced treating professional. Unless all support systems can work together, progress will be limited.

The purpose of this book is to present factual information based on years of experience working with Selectively Mute children, their families, and school personnel and treating professionals.

This book is not a TEXTBOOK, but rather a down-to-earth, easy-to-read GUIDE to helping parents, teachers and treating professionals provide the 'ideal classroom setting for the selectively mute child.'

A personal note to those reading this guidebook: if you come away with just one message, please let it be to approach the SM child with nurturing acceptance, just as I do with each and every child I work with. I have never approached a child from an oppositional standpoint. I firmly believe that the underlying secret to helping SM children, who are truly suffering in silence, is acceptance, understanding and a strong willingness to convey to these children that you genuinely understand their difficulty, and no matter what, you are there for them. Dr. Elisa Shipon-Blum

SELECTIVE MUTISM-STAGES OF SOCIAL COMMUNICATION COMFORT SCALE ©

NON-COMMUNICATIVE -neither non-verbal nor verbal. **NO social engagement.**
STAGE 0 - NO Responding, NO initiating

Child stands motionless (stiff body language), expressionless, averts eye gaze, appears 'frozen,' **MUTE**
OR
Seemingly IGNORES person while interacting or speaking to other(s). **MUTE towards others**

*For communication to occur, <u>Social Engagement</u> must occur

COMMUNICATIVE (Nonverbal and/or Verbal*)
*TO ADVANCE FROM ONE STAGE OF COMMUNICATION TO THE NEXT, INCREASING SOCIAL COMFORT NEEDS TO OCCUR.

STAGE 1 - Nonverbal Communication: (NV)
1A Responding -pointing, nodding, writing, sign language, gesturing, use of 'objects' (e.g. whistles, bells, Non-voice augmentative device (e.g. communication boards/cards, symbols, photos)

1B Initiating -getting someone's attention via pointing, gesturing, writing, use of 'objects' to get attention (e.g. whistles, bells, Non-voice augmentative device (e.g. communication boards/cards, symbols, photos)

STAGE 2 - Transition into Verbal Communication (TV)

2A Responding -Via any <u>sounds,</u> (e.g. grunts, animal sounds, letter sounds, moans, etc.): <u>Verbal Intermediary</u> or Whisper Buddy; <u>Augmentative Device with sound,</u> (e.g. simple message switch, multiple voice message device, tape recorder, video, etc.)

2B Initiating -Getting someone's attention via any <u>sounds,</u> (e.g. grunts, animal sounds, letter sounds, moans., etc.): <u>Verbal Intermediary</u> or Whisper Buddy; <u>Augmentative Device with sound,</u> (e.g. , simple message switch, multiple voice message device ,tape recorder, video, etc)

STAGE 3 - Verbal Communication (VC)

3A Responding – Approximate speech/direct speech (e.g. altered or made-up language, baby talk, reading/rehearsing script, soft whispering, speaking)

3B Initiating - Approximate speech/direct speech (e.g. altered or made-up language, baby talk, reading/rehearsing script, soft whispering, speaking)

A Caring and Understanding Teacher

The ideal teacher for a Selectively Mute child must clearly understand the behavioral characteristics of severely anxious SM children. These children often stand motionless and expressionless and are unable to initiate conversation and play when feeling anxious.

When a teacher asks the SM child a question, the child may just stare back, look away, or put his/her head down. The teacher needs to clearly understand that these behavioral characteristics are due to anxiety and **not** defiance.

The teacher needs to be open-minded and enable the child to communicate in a nonverbal manner. Allowing the child to see that nonverbal communication is accepted relieves pressure and allows the child to feel as though the teacher understands him/her.

Given the opportunity, SM children will become experts in **nonverbal communication!** This can actually be quite fascinating to watch! SM children use a variety of techniques including pointing, tapping, signaling, writing, and often, intricate hand signals to communicate to friends and family when in an anxious setting.

As time goes on, SM children often develop friends with whom they will communicate in the classroom. These other friends also become quite competent in understanding the SM child's 'unspoken' language!

Some examples of simple *nonverbal communication* that the teacher can use to help the SM child are:

Use of hand signals such as thumbs up (yes), thumbs down (no),"OK" signal, etc.

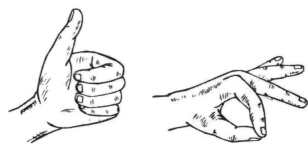

The use of classroom objects. For example, if a child needs to go to the bathroom, wants something for snack, or just wants to say "Hi," a handmade sign can be used.

3x5 cards or larger signs with pre-written messages

Use of word-ring with prewritten words and messages. Child can flip to different words when needing to communicate.

Older children can write answers to questions on a blackboard or in a notebook.

It is important to distinguish between 'enabling' an SM child to remain mute and allowing the child to communicate nonverbally as a means of gaining a sense of 'comfort and stability.' In the beginning stages, such as the start of school or when the child is still anxious and uncomfortable in the classroom, nonverbal communication is used as a way of helping the child become pro-active and relaxed.

Since there are many SM children who may not communicate at all when severely anxious, non-verbal communication is often the first step in 'communication' for many children, and should be looked upon as positive, not negative.

What needs to be determined is the degree of anxiety within the classroom. As the child progresses through treatment, and anxiety is lowered, gradual weaning from nonverbal to verbal communication should be advocated.

> **NOTE: Minimizing direct eye contact towards the child reduces feelings of expectations and anxiety.**

Teachers should allow the younger child to bring in stuffed animals or toys to help them feel more at home. Bringing items from home often gives the child a sense of 'security.' The majority of children tend to leave their special items in their book bags or lockers.

Just knowing their favorite stuffed animal or other 'special item' is close by is often enough to help them feel more comfy in the classroom.

Nurturing & Comfortable Environment

Since the child's level of anxiety is directly influenced by how comfortable he/she feels in any given situation, the teacher must make the SM child feel as comfortable as possible in her classroom setting. Gentle touches, frequent smiling from the teacher, and holding the child's hand when the child obviously is uncomfortable are crucial for an anxious child.

Key for the SM child is to build a sense of comfort within the classroom. This can be accomplished in many different ways.

> Practicing verbalization when few people are around is an excellent way to help your child realize he/she CAN speak in school!

Some examples are:

School personnel should be flexible with the parents and allow them to visit the school before or after hours. Visiting the classroom when few people are around is an excellent way to help the anxious child feel more comfortable. The point is to allow the child to get to know the classroom in a non-threatening and relaxed manner. A suggestion would be for parents to visit the classroom when the teacher is NOT present.

While spending time in the school, with few children and teachers around, parents should encourage verbalization as much as possible. Walk around the school. Go into the library, art and music room. Ask questions, talk about projects. The point is to allow your child to **practice, practice** and **practice** verbalizing! But remember; do not make a 'big deal' about speaking! Parents can certainly praise efforts if the child comments about 'the words coming out,' but if the child is not making a big deal over speaking, by all means, MUM is the word!

This tactic may take some time. At first, the SM child may be silent and seem nervous. As time goes on, the child will become more comfortable, and verbalization will most likely occur.

When the child is in the classroom with the parent before or after school, the child should be allowed to pick and choose what they feel most comfortable doing. Most children will choose to do things that they are too 'scared' or uncomfortable to do when the classroom is filled with children. Place no demands on the child. Allow them to explore and enjoy this one on one time with mom or dad, and at the same time, get to know the classroom in a relaxed fashion.

Allowing the SM child to spend one on one time with the teacher, after hours, is a great way for the teacher and child to get more acquainted with each other. The teacher should go about her own work and let the child explore the classroom. This gets the child used to being near the teacher, but without feeling as if he/she needs to respond or perform. If the child seems 'lost' and needs some direction, presenting the child with puzzles, coloring materials, and just sitting next to the child is a good place to start. As time goes on, and the child has been back to the classroom a few times, the teacher can sit with, read to, and try to interact with the child. **Complimenting the child's work and emphasizing his/her positives is important.** No expectations, whatsoever, should be placed on the child.

Having the teacher visit the child outside of school is another way to help the SM child feel more comfortable. Some families invite the teacher to their home, enabling the child to benefit from the comfort of being in their own environment. This tactic often benefits both the teacher and the child. The teacher gets to know the child in a non-threatening manner and gets to interact one on one, seeing the child in a more relaxed atmosphere. Children often look forward to seeing the teacher outside of school. If the teacher comes to the home, allow the child to take the teacher to his/her room and 'show off' their *stuff.*

The teacher can read, color, and play some games with the child. Verbalization is not the GOAL here. What is important is the comfort level that is being established.

How can a teacher tell if a child is feeling comfortable or if anxiety is heightened? The more anxious, the less communicative and expressive the child will be. For example, a child who stands motionless and/or expressionless when asked a question is MORE anxious than a child who can point, nod or gesture in response to a question. As comfort is established, eye contact will improve; there will be more smiling and less awkward body language.

Suggesting to the child to help decorate the classroom or set up the room for the new school year, or helping to set up for holidays and special events provides the child with extra one on one time in the classroom and with the teacher. This enables the child to feel a sense of 'belonging', and when they see their contributions in the classroom, it is very satisfying and comforting and an excellent self-esteem booster!

SM children will often talk and be relaxed with friends in the comfort of their own environment, such as their own home. However, due to their enhanced anxiety level within the school environment, SM children may not talk to those same children during class or even on the playground.

> Bringing a friend along to the classroom after school or during weekends is an excellent idea! Then two, and eventually three or four children can play and interact in a non-threatening manner

The school should make accommodations for parents to take their child and a special friend to the classroom before or after school when few people are around. With only the SM child and his/her friend present, chances are the SM child will (eventually) speak to his/her friend, and in turn, verbalization may occur during regular school hours!

Question: Should a child be grouped in the same classroom as his/her closest friends? The answer varies. If the SM child is NOT completely dependent on the other children and is not stifling his/her own social development or the other children's, then YES, grouping them together is a wonderful way to help the child feel more comfortable! Communication is most likely to occur with those children with whom the SM child is comfortable.

Flexibility Within the Classroom!

SM children often have difficulty **'initiating & 'responding'** when they are anxious or uncomfortable. There will be times when an SM child cannot complete a task in the classroom   setting. ** Please note that NOT ALL children with SM have this difficulty. Some children perform academic tasks without difficulty or hesitation. However, inability to initiate and respond comfortably may exist in other areas of the child's life.

This is not necessarily a reflection of their lack of knowledge or abilities. This can be very frustrating and embarrassing to the child if they are still working and other children are done and running about. Special planning between the teacher and parent will be necessary to avoid the SM child being left out of discussion or learning time due to their need to finish incomplete tasks.

 **In the classroom setting, there are often tests or situations where 'time limits' are an issue.**

Although this is important in many situations, teachers need to be aware that if it is not absolutely necessary, time limits for the SM child should not be emphasized. When anxious, and not feeling comfortable, Selectively Mute children often have difficulty responding to questions. This is evident by their 'hesitation' in responding. Typically, the SM child will sit there, not react at first, and then slowly begin to perform a task. Their reaction time is slow…almost 'slow-motion' in appearance.

Teachers and school personnel should be alert to this behavior. The child cannot help this reaction. Allowing for more time and understanding that this is not a reflection of either lack of knowledge or defiance is crucial for school personnel to understand.

Presenting a task for the child to perform is a way to determine the degree of anxiety that the child is feeling. The degree begins with:
(1)   MOST ANXIOUS: Unable to respond. Child will sit motionless and often expressionless.
(2)   Child looks at task, may not respond at first, and then very slowly, begins task at hand. Child may look expressionless
(3)   Child responds with hesitation, and then performs the task at a slower than normal pace, but does indeed perform the task without much difficulty. More relaxed body language…
(4)   LEAST ANXIOUS: Child responds normally to task at hand in a timely manner. Child can easily smile and body language is relaxed and carefree.

Teachers should understand that **'hesitation'** is characteristic of Selective Mutism. Time and patience are needed to allow the child to feel as if they are not being rushed. Accommodations should be made to reduce anxiety and thus enable the child to perform a task or answer a question.   Note: please see *'Strategies for Teaching the SM Child'* below.

Strategies for Teaching the SM Child

- SM children need time and patience when being educated.

- Use visual aids and manipulative materials to allow hands-on experience.

- Direct questioning is often difficult and promotes increased anxiety. Be patient, speak slowly, and repeat questioning if necessary.

- Allow adequate time for verbal and nonverbal responses. 'Slow response time' is characteristic of SM children and is not necessarily a reflection of what the child does not know. (The more anxious a child is, the more time needed to respond.)

- SM children are notorious for their difficulty with 'initiating'. Allow for frequent questioning if the SM child looks perplexed or worried.

- Emphasize creativity, imagination, and artistic expression within the classroom and in all subject areas.

- Encourage small group settings, rather than large group discussions.

- Small group discussion should initially be with children with whom the SM child is comfortable. Start with one or two children, and then increase as child's comfort level increases.

- Place SM child's desk next to child or children with whom he/she feels most comfortable.

- Allow SM children to construct, draw, write and/or create when figuring out a problem. Freedom to express helps the SM child convey their knowledge when they are unable to verbalize or respond to direct questioning.

- Use computers, where possible, so that material is presented visually and the child does not feel pressured to speak and respond.

- Assign SM child to a partner, if partners are necessary. Do not wait for SM child to initiate and find a partner.

- If the SM child has difficulty going up to the board to display written answers, the BUDDY SYSTEM can be implemented.

- Allow for a 'Verbal Buddy' in the beginning stages of school and when anxiety is highest. A close friend is an ideal choice!

- When going to lunch, on the play ground, etc…implement the BUDDY SYSTEM if the SM child seems anxious and insecure (evident by stiff body language, lack of eye contact, expressionless face, staring, etc.)

- Goal setting, with the help of a treating professional, should be set up using the child's feelings of comfort as a gauge to what the child can and cannot handle

- Typical progression is in various stages from nonverbal through to verbal. A mute child, barely capable of nonverbal responses cannot be expected to speak. Goals are to help the child progress from nonverbal to verbal communication is

- Verbalization usually begins with the introduction of a verbal intermediary; this is someone to whom the SM child CAN speak comfortably or the use of a 'special friend or object') such as a close friend, parents, stuffed animal, or finger puppet (see below).

A Relaxed, Small Group Setting is BEST!

Since many children with Selective Mutism have social anxiety, a small group setting is IDEAL! In fact, for the majority, small groups are a necessary classroom accommodation to help ease anxiety and to allow progress with comfortable communication (nonverbal and verbal).

Recommendations are to use small group set-ups as much as possible. Suggestions of ways to implement this would be:

-   The buddy system where the child is paired with one other friend, e.g., bathroom buddy, recess buddy, hall buddy. The 'buddy system' is a wonderful way to encourage interaction and communication with one other child without the pressures of a large group.
-   "Lunch Bunch" or "Snack Bunch".
-   Pairing for school projects, field trips, etc.

The more the school can help the child interact and form relationships with other children, the more progress the child is likely to make. Ideally, these 'buddies' should be the same children with whom the parent is arranging play dates or get-togethers, so it is helpful for teachers and parents to discuss the list of children that are being paired.

.

Selectively Mute children may be overly sensitive to loud noises, crowded rooms and bright lights. Therefore, small classroom size in a relaxed atmosphere is ideal. If small classroom size is impossible, then small grouping is preferred for as many group activities as possible.

NOTE: Although not studied officially, preliminary research indicates that a percentage of children with SM have Sensory Processing Disorder

Possible signs of dysfunction of sensory integration are:

1. **Overly sensitive to touch, movement, sights or sounds**
2. **Under-reactive to sensory stimulation**
3. **Activity level that is unusually high or unusually low**
4. **Coordination problems**
5. **Delays in speech or language skills**
6. **Delays in motor skills or academic achievement**
7. **Poor organization of behavior**
8. **A poor self-concept**

If there is a concern about DSI, suggestions would be to talk with your treating professional. He/she may recommend an evaluation by an occupational therapist.

Creative Learning Environment

Children with Selective Mutism are noted for their love of creative expression, such as art and music. By far, art is a favorite among SM children! The typical SM child can draw color and create for hours on end! Since SM children are mute in many settings, they may use art as a means of expressing themselves. Many SM children will choose to do art over most other classroom activities.

Reasons for encouraging art/music are the following:

Success in art/music is an excellent self-esteem booster and can help the child feel successful and special.

Doing 'art' and playing an instrument is a comfort for most SM children and enables them to feel more relaxed in a tense situation.

Can be used as an early 'conversation-booster.' Since SM children are usually very proud of their accomplishments, a teacher can use the child's art/music as a means of talking to the child and complimenting their efforts.

Can be used as a means for the SM child to communicate, i.e. when the teacher asks the child a question, the SM child can draw her/his answer... or play notes that represent certain words!

Art and music can be activities that are emphasized, with the SM child being paired or grouped with other children who love art. Having shared interests is a wonderful way to build social comfort and relationships with other children.

SM children by nature, tend to be more creative in their learning. Reasons for this are still unclear, but it is assumed that the SM child is not able to express him/herself verbally, so instead finds other means of expression, such as music, art, or writing.

A learning atmosphere where a child can learn by experimenting and touching, rather than sequential or pure rote memory is ideal for anxious children. Hands-on learning can 'distract' anxious children by allowing them to focus on the activity rather than their inner feelings.

TESTING

Testing may be needed to assess various academic skills such as school readiness, cognitive (IQ), achievement, speech and language skills, etc.

However, only experienced examiners who understand the anxious child should perform diagnostic testing. Too frequently, examiners mark answers as incorrect, falsely diagnose children with various learning disabilities, and inaccurately measure achievement and cognitive skills, simply because they misinterpret the SM child's responses.

Although most examiners present the testing process in a non-threatening manner, the SM child may still shut down, or freeze, which can dramatically effect his/her response time.

'Testing' the SM child can be misinterpreted and inaccurate because the SM child may:

Be slow-to-respond to directions or questions.

Have difficulty 'initiating' verbal and/or nonverbal responses.

Fail to answer particular questions because of temporary 'freezing' or loss of concentration.

Look away and ignore examiner, as if they do not know the answer.

Teachers and school personnel cannot expect the anxious SM child to respond as other children do to a structured test with strict time limits. Stress levels will often cause inaccurate results, frequently leading to misinterpretation of results, inaccurate results and inappropriate school placement.

Regarding placement for the next school year; shouldn't this be planned early?
Not necessarily! Schools often want to begin the placement and/or IEP development as early as February of the year prior. If a child is involved in a proper treatment program, one month can mean a difference. Therefore, since SM is anxiety, if a clinician, parent and school are working together, the child should make major changes from February till the following August or September. Recommendations are to wait, as long as possible, to make any final determinations. There are many children who are quite severe in February, yet are speakers and communicators within a few months!! Therefore, PATIENCE is key!

Unless necessary, try to limit standardized testing. If testing is a must, then nonverbal and un-timed testing should be used with anxious SM children as much as possible.

School psychologists and teachers often ask how they can test and evaluate the SM child's skills. This is a tricky question to answer because every child is unique. What works for one child does not necessarily work for another child. However, here are suggestions as to how to adequately assess the SM child's abilities:

Have a familiar person administer the evaluations. Certain SM children may have difficulties with nonverbal means of communication with unfamiliar individuals. A suggestion would be for a familiar person to administer the test. If this is not possible, the examiner should try to meet with the child several times prior to the test. Allow the child to sit in the testing room, drawing and coloring or just doing homework, to familiarize him/her with the atmosphere. Another suggestion would be to test the child in his/her own home, or if that is not possible, in the child's classroom.

Presenting the material as a worksheet or fun activity is a subtle way to assess abilities and skills.

If group evaluations are being done, recommendations would be to allow the SM child to be evaluated in a separate room in order to prevent increased anxiety from a large group setting.

Frequent breaks or dividing the evaluation time into separate sessions will often help the SM child feel more relaxed and comfortable.

Allowing for additional time during an evaluation allows the SM child more time to relax and gain a sense of comfort.

VERBAL INTERMEDIARIES!

If a child is mute in school, how can speaking ever really begin?
For some, a close friendship with another child whom the child speaks to at home is enough for verbalization to begin at school. For other, less anxious SM children, as comfort is established from getting to know a child or few children very well at school, verbalization might occur. But, for many, who are mute with everyone in the school, tactics are needed to help transfer speaking into the school environment.

For the child who is comfortably communicating nonverbally (pointing, nodding, writing), the next logical step is to work on transferring speaking into the school. Under the guidance of a treating professional, step-wise tactics can be implemented to enable this to occur with minimal anxiety.

For some children, a stuffed animal, finger puppets, a clenched fist, or another special object can be used as a verbal intermediary.

For younger children, the stuffed animal sits on their desk or can be placed next to the child, or when using finger puppets, the child keeps the puppet on their finger and whispers answers directly to the puppet.   I suggest that the child practice whispering to their 'special friend' at home, in other public settings, and at restaurants and stores, so that whispering to their special friend in school is an easy transition. As children get older, they become much more self-conscious about using intermediaries, such as stuffed toys, puppets, etc. For older children, use of a clenched fist, one finger, or a finger puppet hidden in the palm of the hand is more appropriate.

Using a parent or close friend as a verbal intermediary is another way to transfer speaking into the school. Suggestions would be for the child to spend time in the classroom with just his/her parent, or the parent and a close friend. The idea is that with few other people present, the child will often be able to speak. Using this tactic under the guidance of a treating professional, and without pressuring the child to speak, often creates a relatively anxiety free way to introduce speaking into school!

How to use a verbal intermediary: The SM child whispers to the verbal intermediary up close. The verbal intermediary then transfers the words to the other person (obviously if stuffed animals or other objects are used as the verbal intermediary, the other person needs to wait until further distance away is accomplished so that they can HEAR the words, but in the beginning, just allowing the child to whisper to the intermediary is KEY).

The goal here is that as the child becomes more and more comfortable whispering at a certain distance he/she will then move to the next distance, until eventually, VOILA!!! ---The child is speaking to the other person!

> **Using the child's feelings as a gauge, whispering up close, then progressing to fist length→ half an arm length→ full arm length→ across a table are the stages of 'distance' that whispering occurs.***
>
> **For many SM children, making eye contact or even looking toward another person is very difficult. As whispering is occurring comfortably via the intermediary, goals should be implemented to gradually encourage 'looking toward' the other person when answering. Eye contact is something that cannot be pushed but will, over time, occur.**
>
> *** These goals should be planned under the guidance of a treating professional to assure that the child is READY to progress forward. If a child is 'pushed' when not ready, heightened anxiety will occur.**

Prepare the Child for Changes

It is important that routines are followed through as much as possible. **children with SM need consistency and routine**! Any changes in the schedule should be planned ahead of time, if possible.

Ways to prepare child for change:

> "Anxious children do not do well with unexpected changes"

Talk with the child and explain the change ahead of time.

Prepare as far ahead as possible for change. For example, if the child is going on a field trip, or if a substitute teacher will be in the classroom, adequate notice will often prevent an array of uncomfortable repercussions.

Speak with the child's parents about 'anticipated' changes so that the parents can help prepare the child as well.

In addition, if the regular teacher is to be out of school one day, it is wise for the school administration to inform the substitute about the SM child's needs. A recommendation would be for the regular classroom teacher to have notes already written and prepared so the substitute can be made aware of the SM child's needs. Unfortunately, one day of an uninformed or unaccepting teacher can push the child back months of progress!

> Obviously there are times when change is completely unexpected. Such is life, and the SM child must learn to deal with these events. In these situations it is helpful for the teacher involved to do a bit more hand holding, smiling and giving reassurance to ALL children affected by unexpected change. As time goes on, children will learn to adapt to the punches that life tends to throw at us every once in a while!

Another unexpected change is if the SM child's closest friend is absent from school. This obviously can occur and can't be prevented. This can be quite difficult, though, for the anxious child who feels ALONE and isolated without his/her friend in class. Recommendations are for the teacher to try to offer support and comfort to the child, and perhaps make an effort to pair or group the child with his/her 'next best friend'.'

Remember, too, that the more comfortable the SM child is within the class, the better they are likely to react to changes. The majority of SM children will begin to adapt well as long as a gentle hand is close by!

Possible Dilemmas

Toileting

SM children, especially younger children, notoriously have issues with **toileting** in school. Since they are unable to speak, and frequently have tremendous difficulty with 'initiating,' they often cannot go up to the teacher to indicate the need to use the bathroom.

It is important for the teacher of a young SM child to let the child know the various ways he/she can communicate the need to use the bathroom in school.

Many children will go all day without using the bathroom! This can lead to:
- Accidents (causing embarrassment and humiliation)
- Urinary infections
- Kidney damage - This is rare, but has occurred (where urine 'refluxes' back up into the kidneys)

Recommendations to help the child become comfortable using the bathroom in school would be to:

- Allow parents to spend time before or after school with the child. Parents can initially take the child to the bathroom, and as time goes on, gradually suggest (using a form of positive reinforcement with rewards) that the child go alone.
- Pair the child with a *'bathroom buddy.'*
- Have scheduled bathroom times within the classroom.
- Teachers can give the SM child an <u>object</u> that is representative of their need 'to go'.
- Allow the child to use <u>hand signals</u> to indicate they need to use the bathroom.
- Allow the child to <u>write a note</u>, or <u>draw a picture</u> to notify the teacher of their need 'to go.'

Eating

Selectively Mute children may have difficulty with *eating* in school.

One of the traits of social phobia is embarrassment when eating in front of others. SM children are also known to manifest this tendency. In many cases, the child may refuse to eat all together, try to hide and eat, or wait until other children are finished and away from the table.

The teacher needs to communicate to the parents if eating is an issue so that discussions on how to handle this can be held.

Teachers and parents should realize that the child's difficulty with eating in front of others is a DIRECT result of an anxiety disorder, NOT DEFIANCE!

Recommendations to help the SM child feel more comfortable with eating in school would be to:

- Allow the parents to bring in food during snack time. Allow mom or dad to join the child in the cafeteria.
- After a few days, parents can start getting up and leaving the table earlier & earlier, until eventually, they no longer have to be there!
- Encourage small groups at lunch tables, or allow the child to sit with just one or two children whom he/she feels most comfortable.

Despite using all of these tactics, there will be a proportion of children who will *not* eat in school. Recommendations are to NOT make a 'big deal' over this. In these cases, if the child needs some 'alone' time to eat, and then the school should allow for this. For younger SM children, the above recommendations to build comfort with the school is usually enough to stimulate eating within the school environment.

Fire Drills

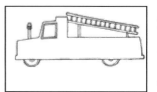 Fire drills are often unexpected and can be quite frightening to all children. Imagine the feelings a mute child may be experiencing! Advice would be to practice fire drills without the loud bell. Literally go through the 'act' and explain exactly what needs to be done during a fire drill. Then, let the child HEAR the loud noise, so when a fire drill does occur, the loud sound will be expected.

Recess Can be Tough for the SM Child

Most children love recess and cannot wait to play outside and run around with friends! But for the anxious child, recess can be a time that is dreaded and brings on an array of anxious feelings. SM children fear embarrassing themselves, whether by falling, 'looking foolish' or being left out of the group.

A Favorite Playground Activity for SM Children is swinging. Some children with SM feel safe on the swings. Since initiating play and verbalizing is difficult for the SM child, 'swinging' next to another child may be the SM child's only way of interacting with other children

Socializing

As mentioned, SM children often have difficulty **initiating**. As a result, their ability to socialize with other children may be greatly affected. It usually takes an assertive child to initiate with the SM child to begin playing. The SM child may stand alone or seem withdrawn, not because of their choosing, but because of their INABILITY to initiate with others. By nature, SM children are very social beings. They want to interact with others, but often have a great deal of difficulty doing so. Therefore, some encouragement, by taking the child's hand, helping them to interact or PAIRING the child with another child is a wonderful way to help the child build comfort and to encourage socialization.

Frequently Asked Questions!

1. <u>Should children with Selective Mutism be placed in the regular classroom or within a *special education* class?</u>
For the majority of Selectively Mute children, mainstreaming in the regular classroom is appropriate and necessary! Proper socialization and meeting the demands of the academics should be instilled from the beginning. Unless there are other prevailing factors that warrant removing the SM child from the classroom (such as severe learning disabilities or other issues that are causing an interruption in proper learning and socializing), accommodating the child in the regular classroom is of utmost importance. SM children are anxious, but with the guidance of a proper treatment strategy developed by a competent professional, the school and parents can work as a team to build comfort and confidence and these children should progress quite positively. This may be accomplished in part with special accommodations within the classroom setting. Children with Selective Mutism tend to be intelligent, sensitive, introspective and perceptive, and can not only gain quite a bit from the classroom setting, but can be an asset as well. Their insights, creativity, love for learning, and intelligence can and should be nurtured within the regular classroom setting.

2. <u>How is school phobia related to Selective Mutism?</u>
Selectively Mute children have an innate 'fear' and/or 'anxiety' when in social settings, such as school. In response to this, some SM children may try to avoid school. This can be due to physical symptoms that often accompany anxiety symptoms. Stomachaches, nausea, headaches, etc., can make SM children want to avoid school in order to relieve their symptoms. Fears of embarrassment, social interaction, making mistakes, changing in gym class, etc., are enough to cause many SM children to beg to stay home. Over time, these children, if left untreated, may try to avoid going to school or to other social events as a means of alleviating their anxiety. They realize, whether subconsciously or consciously, that they feel calmer and more relaxed in the comfort of their own home or away from the stress that they feel in the school setting. Parents may have a difficult time getting the child

to school or may be reluctant to send their child to school in case they are truly ill.

3. <u>What are IDEA and IEP and how do these relate to children with SM?</u>
IDEA (Individuals with Disabilities Education Act) is federal legislation that protects students with disabilities. This includes SM students from ages 3-21 years old who, due to their severe anxiety and/or their inability to speak are having problems with learning and socialization within the classroom setting.

There are two parts to IDEA:
- SPECIAL EDUCATION – An individualized teaching program for an SM child should focus on accommodations to help decrease anxiety, build self-esteem, and to increase confidence in social settings. **Focus should not be on verbalization**. Pushing a child to speak will only backfire and push a child backwards. When anxiety is low enough, and a comfort level has been reached, verbalization will often follow or verbal goals can be set under the guidance of an experienced treating professional.
- ADDITIONAL SERVICES - support services a child may need to help him learn. (Examples are small group settings (counseling, speech therapy), parent training, a one-to-one aide, or use of equipment such as a tape recorder.
- IDEA describes in detail the multi-disciplinary evaluation procedures required to determine if a child is eligible for special education, as well as the requirement that the child be reevaluated at least every three years, using the same procedures. For the child evaluated for governmental service under IDEA, a meeting with the parents must be arranged at least once per year in order to develop an IEP (Individualized Education Plan) for the student. The IEP describes the special education and related services that the child will receive.

4. How is Section 504 different from IDEA?

Section 504 does not require a written IEP, and protects *a broader* based program that affects many more children than IDEA. In the case of the SM child, the child's school provides a 504 plan in order to protect the child in the classroom by providing ways to lower anxiety, build self-esteem and increase confidence in social settings. Section 504 requires schools to make "reasonable accommodations;' such as letting a child pair with another child for certain school activities, permitting small group lessons for one child instead of requiring participation in large groups, and allowing a child to tape record lessons or to use notes as a means of nonverbal communication.

5. Are either a 504 or IEP necessary for the SM child?

Depending upon the severity of the child's social communication deficit as well as the possibility that other factors (Speech and language, sensory processing, etc) <u>affect the child's ability to function and learn</u> within the classroom should dictate which plan should be used. The more affected a child is in terms of their 'disability' the more an IEP may be necessary.

For the milder child who is starting/completing work on time, participating in a group and benefiting from the educational programs, then a 504 plan may be necessary to help with basic accommodations and necessary interventions to build the social comfort and to progress communicatively. However, there are certain children, especially older grade school SM children who have been mute for many years, that may need a more structured and regimented plan to help accommodate their needs. In these cases, an IEP may be more appropriate.

Speech services or psychological services are ideal for many SM children because these provide an opportunity to develop a comfort level with a small group of children or one on one with a counselor. In some districts, to acquire such services, an IEP may be necessary.

The bottom line is the child with SM needs HELP within the school. Whether the plan is called an IEP, 504 or 'SHMI-E-P' does not truly matter, as long as the child has the PROPER accommodations and interventions to allow him/her to build the social comfort, progress communicatively and to LEARN within the classrooms setting.

As this comfort level builds, the therapist could gradually add some children from the classroom into the session. As the child develops a comfort level with other children from the class, tactics can be used to help this carry over into the regular classroom.

Typical accommodations for children with SM are listed below.

- Allowing the parents to spend time with the SM child in the school environment before school, after school and on weekends to allow for desensitization and the practice of verbalization with few individuals present. Parents should be encouraged to walk the halls, visit classrooms, cafeteria, etc., allowing the SM child to develop an increased comfort level in the school environment.
- Promoting small group activities (in contrast to large group) with close friends.
- Pairing SM child with a 'bathroom or eating buddy.'
- Pairing the SM child with a partner for classroom discussions.
- Allowing the SM child to write answers to questions, instead of requiring verbal responses.
- Allowing the SM child to use hand signals to indicate their needs or answers to questions.
- Instituting 'Board buddies' where SM children can be accompanied by a buddy to the blackboard or front of the class.
- Scheduling one-on-one time with the teacher, counselor or psychologist and then with one or two other close friends.
- Allowing the child to TAPE RECORD lessons at home and/or alone in the classroom.
- Allowing the parents to help out within the classroom as much as possible to increase the child's comfort level. Experience proves that the SM child will whisper to the parents rather rapidly, and over some time, with guidance, this can carry over to verbalization.

**Special accommodations are designed to provide the opportunity for selectively mute children to develop a comfort level within the classroom and create an optimal educational experience.

6. <u>What is the assessment and evaluation process for a child suspected of having SM?</u>
A trained professional familiar with Selective Mutism should interview the child's parents. Emphasis will be on social interaction and developmental history, as well as behavioral characteristics (including any delays in hearing, speech and language), family history (history of family members with anxiety/depression is common), behavioral characteristics (shy characteristics, inhibited temperament), home life description (family stress, divorce, death, etc.), and medical history. After evaluating the results of the initial interview, the professional will often see the child. Although many SM children do not speak to the diagnosing professional, the professional can spend time with the child and attempt to build trust and assess the child for interaction and communication abilities, etc. Given time and patience, the typical SM child should be able to communicate to the clinician via eye contact, body language, facial expressions, written expression, etc. Because 20-30 % of selectively mute children have a subtle abnormality with speech and language, a thorough speech and language evaluation is often ordered if there is a question. In addition, a complete physical exam (including hearing,) standardized testing, psychological assessments, as well as a thorough developmental screening are often recommended if the diagnosis is still not clear. Video tapes of the child interacting at home or in another comfortable setting can often prove useful to verify that the child is indeed verbalizing normally in at least one environment.

7. <u>Are academic assessments necessary for the SM child?</u>
Again, every child is unique, so each circumstance is different. Anxiety can mask other disorders and visa versa; therefore careful attention to academic issues is important in order to rule in or rule out other concomitant disorders (see question 8.) Anxiety can most certainly affect cognitive function and achievement.

Anxiety can be crippling, causing the SM child to 'shut down' within the classroom. This is manifested when the child is unable to complete certain classroom worksheets or assignments, and is slow to respond and/or has an inability to initiate responses (either verbally or nonverbally), poor school performance, inattentiveness, etc. Teachers and psychologists should meet with the parents to discuss concerns about academic performance if the child is unable to perform appropriately. Careful attention to the child's ability to perform in a comfortable setting, such as home, is important. Parents may indicate that the child 'rattles off answers' and 'whips out homework rapidly and successfully, with minimal effort' when at home. If this is the case, a suggestion might be to allow the SM child to take home grade-appropriate work. Then it can be assumed that the ANXIETY is causing the child's inability to perform within the classroom. If this is the case, as it is with the majority of Selectively Mute children, then remedial work is not appropriate, nor are special services to help the child with academic skills. What is appropriate; however, are accommodations to lower anxiety within the classroom. This can be accomplished by teachers working concurrently with a specialist who has developed an individualized treatment plan for the child.

8. If academic assessments are needed, how should the evaluations be done for the SM child?
The examiner should understand that the SM child needs more time to adjust and relax to perform an evaluation. SM children are notorious for hesitancy and an inability to initiate, so time restraints should be avoided whenever possible. Recommendations are to use non-timed nonverbal tests to assess knowledge. Allow the child to practice a similar test or 'worksheet' within the regular classroom or perhaps at home. Ideally the test should be administered at the child's home or in a familiar classroom; it is not unheard of that examiners will visit the child at home a few times, and then perform the test within the home environment! If these options are not possible then recommendations would be to allow the SM child to spend quite a bit of time, a few days prior to the examination, getting used to the examiner's room. There are various nonverbal assessment tests (The Bracken nonverbal test, the UNIT, LEITER and TONI IQ test,

etc.) that can be used with the SM child to evaluate their skills and abilities. However, patience and an understanding and nurturing attitude from the examiner are crucial for the SM child to perform, and even then, results may be inaccurate and unreliable unless anxiety is low. Body language, amount of eye contact, facial expressions, etc., are subtle ways the examiner can determine the anxiety status of the SM child. A smiling, cheerful, relaxed-looking child is more likely to perform up to his/her true ability and test results can be interpreted as more accurate than with a stiff, expressionless child who is unable to make eye contact.

9. <u>What is the school psychologist's role in helping the SM child?</u>
When a child is mute in school, a classroom teacher will often go to the school psychologist for help. The psychologist needs to be able to recognize Selective Mutism (SM), differentiate symptoms from other disorders, and know how to best help the SM child effectively in the classroom. The school psychologist's role is to:
- Aid the classroom teacher in finding the best way to educate, manage and properly socialize the Selectively Mute Child. (Recommending small group interaction, nonverbal means of communication, etc.)
- Guide the parents through the correct channels for the child to receive proper evaluation and an effective treatment plan.
- Coordinate the collaborative efforts among the treating clinician, teacher and parents to best help the SM child.
It is of utmost importance for everyone to be in continuous contact with regard to the SM child's progress. Frequent "tweaking" of the treatment plan needs to be done in order to find the best tactics that work for a particular child. The school psychologist is often in the best position to coordinate these efforts.

10. <u>Is it appropriate for older children to TAPE their lessons from home, and then allow the teacher to hear the tape?</u>
Taping lesson plans, whether it is via video or audiotape, is appropriate, assuming that there is a goal in place for a gradual weaning to 'verbalization'. For example, a teacher might allow the child to tape his/her lessons at home, and then encourage the child to tape in a classroom (with only a parent present). The next

step would be to encourage the child to tape in a classroom without parent present, and then encourage him/her to tape part of lesson, then whisper lesson to parent (or teacher) within the class setting. Further along would be to whisper the entire school lesson within the classroom with only teacher present, increase to a few students plus teacher, and at a later stage increase to all verbalization. Ideally taping should be used when a child needs to present academic material to a teacher, as an accommodation for the child's inability to speak.

11. Why do SM children seem to have such difficulty communicating and ultimately verbalizing to the teacher?
It can actually be quite easy to understand if one considers that the child views the teacher as the ultimate authority figure who has an **expectation** of him/her to perform and participate. This can be quite frightening to the child who suffers from social anxiety. Up until the time the child enters school, parents are the main authority figures in the child's life (for the most part), and upon entering school, the SM child feels the immediate expectation as soon as they enter the classroom. The teacher asks questions, makes rules, organizes and leads the classroom activities. The role the teacher fills is quite scary to the anxious child who is completely overwhelmed and fearful of his/her ability to perfom in this social setting. The teacher of the SM child needs to convey, early on, that there is absolutely no pressure to **talk.**

12. What is the best treatment for Selective Mutism?
An individualized treatment plan should be designed by a professional who understands Selective Mutism. This can be a physician and/or therapist, such as a social worker, psychologist, etc. Treatment should not focus on getting the child to speak, but rather, to **lower overall anxiety, build self-esteem and increase confidence and communication in social settings.** The best treatment seems to be a combination of behavioral therapy with/without medication. Some children, particularly younger ones, progress well with appropriate behavioral therapy. In other cases, medication is prescribed to lower initial anxiety levels. In as little as a few days after beginning medications such as the Selective Serotonin Reuptake Inhibitors (SSRI's), parents often see a difference in their child's behaviors. Parents commonly

state seeing more eye contact, less awkward body language, and improved behavioral flexibility. Medication should never be used alone, but should be part of an overall treatment plan and when used, the goal is to remain on the medication for 9-12 months. Medication helps lower anxiety levels enough to do the behavioral treatment necessary to build long lasting coping skills and to overcome Selective Mutism. When Selective Mutism is approached from this perspective, children usually progress quite positively!

13. What if a child has to give an oral presentation? How would that be handled?

Depending on the age of the child, he/she can use the buddy system where a friend can read or present the oral presentation. The child can tape their lesson at home and then play it for the class, or the teacher can listen alone. The student can also write their presentation and the teacher or friend can read the presentation to the class. As time goes on, and comfort is established, positive reinforcement, fading, modeling, and desensitization techniques should be implemented in order to gradually help the child progress into verbalization. Under the guidance of an experienced professional, SM children will make progress. Time and patience are required, however. Attempting to rush the process will only backfire by increasing the child's anxiety, causing regression rather than progress.

14. Should a child be 'held back' in school if SM is her/his only problem?

Absolutely not! Stifling a bright, creative, inquisitive child by holding them back is inappropriate and unacceptable. If an SM child is not making steady progress, a reevaluation of the child's treatment plan should be done immediately. Unfortunately, a large number of schools base the decision on whether to allow the child to progress to the next grade level by 'mutism' alone. This should not be the case. Nonverbal assessments and evaluations should be used to determine the child's readiness from a cognitive and achievement standpoint. However, it must be stressed again that evaluating the SM child should accommodate for anxiety as much as possible and testing must be interpreted with caution. Testing is often inaccurate or misleading (see section on testing).

Also, schools will often suggest evaluations in early spring for the next school year. If a child is in a productive treatment program, social readiness and 'anxiety levels' should change considerably from month to month, especially for the younger children. One month can make a world of difference. Therefore recommendations are to hold off on making a decision about promoting or retaining a child as long as possible!

15.   If an SM child needs discipline, how should that be done without making the child shut down or feel singled out?
If an SM child is doing something inappropriate within the classroom, they should be disciplined just like any other child. Special treatment for the SM child is not fair to either the SM child or the other children in the class. In fact, if other children feel the SM child is receiving special treatment, they will often resent him/her. The teacher should therefore calmly discipline the child in an appropriate manner, keeping in mind that all children benefit from firm but positive discipline that shows limits and expectations without causing humiliation or embarrassment.

16.   If a teacher asks an SM child a question, and the child turns away, does not respond, or takes a long time to respond isn't this oppositional and defiant behavior?
Not necessarily. As mentioned throughout the book, depending on the degree of anxiety, some SM children may not even be able to respond nonverbally. In other cases, children with SM may respond, but anxiety may cause a 'hesitation' in response. If the child is sitting there without a smile, and unable to make appropriate eye contact, chances are the child is feeling too anxious and is unable to respond comfortably. In fact, this is quite characteristic of the way many SM children respond to authority figures like teachers - particularly if someone is expecting 'too much' from the child. Turning away, ignoring, or 'just staring' is an SM child's reaction to feeling anxious and stressed and these children are literally unable to respond appropriately. The teacher should NOT view this as defiance or rudeness. When a child responds by turning away or ignoring the teacher, the teacher should take it as a sign that the child is feeling anxious and needs a bit more hand-holding, comforting and reassuring. It is a

mistake to assume that the child is being difficult or controlling simply because the child may have been interacting comfortably with a friend, perhaps laughing, whispering and talking prior to demonstrating non-communicative behavior with the teacher. As anxiety is lowered, the child will eventually begin to respond to the teacher. However, other methods should be used in the interim to help the child communicate, such as asking the child to LOOK in the direction of the correct answer. If the child still cannot perform, recommendations are to praise the child for 'trying' and to mention this to the parent and/or treating professional.

17.   What should a teacher do if a SM child freezes and won't move?

This happens quite frequently, especially with younger children and/or in the beginning of the school year. Mornings are difficult, as is returning to school after an illness or vacation. The teacher should greet the child just as they do any other child. If the SM child is standing in one place, not moving and looking expressionless, recommendations would be for the teacher to take the child's hand and direct him/her where he/she needs to go.   It is unusual for a child to stay 'frozen-looking' for an extended period of time. Many SM children love to draw and create. Suggestions would be to ease anxiety by directing the child to a table or desk and allowing him/her to draw or color. In the majority of cases, the SM child will go with the teacher and be relieved to sit and draw before making a transition to other activities.

18.   After an SM child is speaking to children in the classroom, how do you carry that over to the teacher?

Again, this takes time and patience. Verbalization will not occur until the child's internal anxiety level is lowered. With a proper treatment plan in place, there should be instructions and tactics by the treating clinician to help the child become more comfortable with the teacher. Advice would be for the teacher to spend quite a bit of one on one time with the child before and after school. Perhaps the teacher will visit the child outside of school.   The point is to take all pressure off the child. The teacher should have **no expectation** of verbalization from the child.   Interestingly enough, when the teacher's expectations are lowered and emphasis is on building trust and establishing a comfort level with the child, verbalization will usually follow.

19. What should a teacher tell the SM child's classmates when they ask why the SM child doesn't talk?

This happens quite often. Recommendations would be to have all the children write a list of the things that make them scared or afraid. Then explain to the children that this is how their friend (the SM child) feels about speaking; that it is scary and very difficult for him/her, but that everyone can help him/her by not asking them questions or making comments about 'not talking.'

20. If a child is completely mute within the classroom, will verbalization automatically begin when anxiety is lowered?

This is not an easy question to answer. The answer is YES & NO. YES, assuming SPECIFIC techniques and tactics are used to lower anxiety; such as desensitization, modeling, fading, positive reinforcement and perhaps cognitive-behavioral therapy, with/without medication. The purposeful tactics enable progress with communication comfort, hence speaking. If anxiety is lowered, without adequately building the necessary coping skills, communication and ultimately verbalization will be limited.
NO, because unless the above techniques and tactics are 'put together' in a purposeful manner and there is a way to transfer speaking INTO the school setting, communication progression and verbalization will be stifled and limited. In addition, unless coping skills are built, a child may regress, revert or make limited progress with communication.

21. How can verbalization be transferred into the school setting?

A very successful tactic is the use of a verbal intermediary! This can be a parent, close friend, or even a stuffed animal that the child can begin to whisper to in school. Communication through a verbal intermediary is started with whispering close up to other person (or object), at fist-length away, half arm length away, full arm length away, and then from across the table. This is accomplished with child's FULL support using goal setting with positive reinforcement based on the child's comfort level. Beginning verbalization via goals when the child is TOO anxious will only sabotage progress. The child's treating professional should help gauge 'readiness' for this goal.

22. What if the child CANNOT speak to anyone within the school setting, how can speaking ever really occur?
This is a typical concern and question among educators, parents and treating professionals. To help with introduction of verbalization within the school setting, the use of a verbal intermediary to help TRANSFER speaking into the school will help immensely! Careful planning where the child spends time alone in the school with the person(s) whom the child is MOST comfortable with outside of school is crucial to this process of building 'verbal' comfort within the school setting. This is usually a parent or perhaps a close friend whom the child speaks to comfortably outside of school. Parents spending time before or after school when few children are present is a wonderful way to begin this process! Working with a treating professional to gauge anxiety and to help progress forward will enable this process to continue and extend into the classroom with other children and school personnel.

23. What if a teacher and school personnel recognize that the child may have Selective Mutism, but the parents are in denial and believe the child is 'just shy' and will outgrow their silence?
Unfortunately, this scenario occurs all too often. It must be understood that parents get such conflicting advice from doctors, friends and family members, often being told that their child is "just shy" and will outgrow this behavior. It is helpful for the teachers and school administrators to call a meeting between parents and one or two school personnel (so as not to overwhelm the parents.) Prior to the meeting, school personnel are encouraged to gather as much information as possible about Selective Mutism. Careful attention not to alienate the parents is vital. Presenting information to back-up belief that SM is a possible diagnosis is key. Perhaps a first meeting to introduce the concept and present the parents with information (such as the handout "When the Word's Just Won't Come Out," available via the free download page of the SMG~CAN website) is one way to begin introducing the idea. Direct the family to the SMG~CAN website for further information. Obviously, there are going to be

many parents, who despite having all information in front of them, will still be in denial or insist that your intuition is incorrect. The school can only hope that the parents will eventually realize the importance of an early diagnosis and treatment. Unfortunately, without parental support, the child has little chance of making significant progress to overcome their SM.

24.   <u>What if a child has been on medication for some time, looks more relaxed, but speaking has not occurred within school or other social settings?</u>
This scenario happens far too often. The main reasons for this are:
-        Depending on medication alone to 'make the child speak.'
-        No formal treatment approach to enable for progress and coping skills.
What needs to be understood is that mutism becomes ingrained behavior, and that unless specific tactics and techniques are introduced, this behavior cannot easily be unlearned. Therefore, even if the child is taking medication, but there are no tools to help them UNLEARN the mute and often minimally communicative behavior, progress will reach a certain point and then become limited and stifled.

25.   <u>Where can parents, teachers and psychologists turn for additional help with understanding Selective Mutism?</u>

The Selective Mutism Anxiety Research and Treatment Center offers Evaluations, Treatment, IEP and 504 plan development, as well as webinars, workshops, conferenes and a variety of products and other services, etc. <u>www.selectivemutismcenter.org</u>

The Selective Mutism Group-Childhood Anxiety Network (SMG~CAN) at <u>www.selectivemutism.org</u> is primarily a member-based organization that is an excellent resource for all interested in learning about Selective Mutism. The SMG~CAN is the world's leading source of information on this childhood anxiety disorder.

Working as a Team

The most successful approach to helping the anxious Selectively Mute child is for parents, teacher, treating professional and other relevant professionals to work together as a team. The support of the school and parents in the treatment plan for the child is crucial. Progression from nonverbal to verbal communication is accomplished by basing goals on the child's comfort level. It should be noted that an individual treatment plan should also focus on the REAL WORLD. In addition to increasing comfort in school, goals should be set forth to help the child cope at parties, in restaurants, malls, doctor's offices, etc. Making phone calls and being able to initiate with others is crucial to the child's overall well-being and ability to function successfully in life.

"An 'ideal classroom setting' can make a world of difference in the SM child's ability to successfully overcome communication anxiety. Recommendations are for the parents, teacher, and other school personnel who will come into contact with the SM child to learn as much as possible about the childhood anxiety disorder, Selective Mutism. Unfortunately, there is inaccurate and very misleading literature in print that portrays the SM child as oppositional, controlling, defiant, 'just shy,' etc. Facts are that SM children are not oppositional by nature; they are not 'just shy.' They are truly incapacitated by their anxiety to the point of dysfunction. Coping skills to combat anxiety are inadequate. Because of this, mutism often becomes learned and difficult to overcome unless an experienced treating professional can work hand in hand with parents, child and school personnel to progress forward in a stepwise fashion to lower anxiety build self-esteem and increase confidence and communication within the school setting.

With the proper treatment plan in place, understanding and dedicated parents, a nurturing school environment, and a loving and caring teacher, the SM child will be well on their way to overcoming Selective Mutism and succeeding and enjoying school!" *Dr. E*

ABOUT THE AUTHOR:

Elisa Shipon-Blum DO is the President & Director of the Selective Mutism Anxiety Research and Treatment Center (SMART-Center) located in NE Philadelphia, Pennsylvania. She is the Founder & Director Emeritus of the Selective Mutism Group Childhood Anxiety Network. (SMG~CAN).

In addition, Dr Shipon-Blum is Clinical Assistant Professor of Psychology & Family Medicine at the Philadelphia College of Osteopathic Medicine. She is a board certified family physician who specializes in Selective Mutism.

Dr Shipon-Blum practices in Philadelphia, PA and has developed Social Communication Anxiety Treatment (SCAT) from her years studying & researching individuals with Selective Mutism. She consults worldwide with families, treating professionals and educators and has helped countless children from around the world overcome Selective Mutism.

Dr. Shipon-Blum lectures throughout the country on the topic of Selective Mutism, performs school evaluations and trainings for treating professionals, educators & parents and is considered one of the world's leading experts in the treatment and understanding of Selective Mutism.

Dr. E has been a featured expert on national television shows such as CNN, Inside Edition, Good Morning America as well as other local TV and Radio broadcasts. In addition, she has been featured in TIME Magazine (Feb 6th, 06) and has interviewed with newspapers such as the NEW York Times, Chicago Tribune, Boston Globe, San Diego Tribune, Phila. Inquirer, Palm Beach Post and multiple other national/local media. Dr. E is also a featured expert for a range of international media outlets such a radio, TV and newspapers.

Dr. Shipon-Blum is presently involved in multiple collaborative research projects with top researchers and clinicians and has written numerous articles and books on Selective Mutism and anxiety including: 'Easing School Jitters for the Selectively Mute child,' The Ideal Classroom Setting for the Selectively Mute child,' 'Understanding Katie' (a book series about a little girl with Selective mutism), 'Supplement Treatment Guide Book to Understanding Katie' and 'Selective Mutism and Social Anxiety Disorder in School.'

Dr. Shipon-Blum (or Dr. E as her patients refer to her) prides herself on being 'down to earth' and 'easy to speak to', and resides with her four young children, husband and 'multiple' dogs in the NE suburbs of Philadelphia, Pennsylvania.

3057548

Made in the USA